ANCIENT GREECE

Anne Millard

Illustrated by Joseph McEwan
and Sue Stitt

Designed by Kim Blundell
Edited by Jane Chisholm

Contents

First published in 1981 by Usborne Publishing Ltd. Usborne House, 83-85 Saffron Hill, London EC1N8RT, England

Copyright © 1987, 1981 Usborne Publishing Ltd.

The name Usborne and the device 🐝 are Trade Marks of Usborne Publishing Ltd.

Printed in Italy

About this Book

This book is packed with colourful pictures and information which tell you what life was like in Ancient Greece. There are lots of scenes, like this one of people at the theatre, which have been reconstructed from archaeological and written evidence.

Sometimes, instead of a reconstructed scene, you will see a reproduction of a Greek painting or carving. The paintings mostly come from Greek pots, which were often decorated with scenes from daily life.

There are also detailed illustrations of things the Greeks used, such as furniture, tools, jewellery and weapons. Some are based on objects shown in paintings or described in books, but most show things that can still be seen today.

The history of Ancient Greece is divided into "Ages" and "Periods". You can find out what these are in the chart on page 5. This book concentrates on life in the Classical Period, although there are references to the Archaic and Hellenistic Periods too. For an outline of the history of Ancient Greece and its key personalities, see pages 60-61.

Greece in this period was divided into independent city states. This book concentrates on Athens, which was the largest and most powerful, although much of the information applies to the other states as well. Sparta is considered separately, as many customs there were different from the rest of Greece.

You may want to see some Ancient Greek objects and ruins for yourself. On page 62, there is a list of museums with good Greek collections, as well as sites in Greece.

The map on pages 58-59 shows you where many of the places are that are mentioned in the book.

3

Introduction to Ancient Greece

The history of Greece can be traced back to Stone Age hunters. Later came early farmers and the civilizations of the Minoan and Mycenaean kings. This was followed by a period of wars and invasions, known as the Dark Ages. In about 1100BC, a people called the Dorians invaded from the north and spread down the west coast. In the period discussed in this book – about 500–336BC – Greece was divided into small city states, each of which consisted of a city and its surrounding countryside.

This map shows the main
provinces and islands
of Ancient Greece.

The land

Greece is a hot, dry, mountainous country. The hills were probably more wooded in ancient times than they are now. Good farming land was limited to narrow valleys and coastal plains. People were never far from the sea, so it played an important part in their lives. The Greek coastline is full of inlets and bays and there are many islands.

4

The people

In the Classical Period, most Greek city states had governments that were democratically elected by the citizens. Not all the inhabitants were citizens, however. Excluded from citizenship were all women, foreigners, slaves and freed slaves. Slaves were usually prisoners of war, or people born of slave parents.

A citizen and his wife   Foreigners

Slaves

How we know about the Ancient Greeks

Useful evidence can be drawn from ancient buildings. Some of these are still standing, although in ruins, others have been excavated by archaeologists. Carvings and paintings on buildings sometimes record historical events, as well as myths and legends.

The writings of Greek historians, philosophers, poets and playwrights have taught us a great deal about how people lived and thought.

Pottery is an important source of information. Changes in the shapes and designs help archaeologists to date the sites where pots are found and learn more about where the Greeks traded. Paintings on the pots tell us about their lives and their traditional stories.

Chart of main periods

c.*6000-2900BC	Neolithic Period
c.2900-2000BC	Early Bronze Age
c.2000-1400BC	Minoan Age (on the island of Crete)
c.1600-1100BC	Mycenaean Age (on mainland)
c.1100-750BC	The Dark Ages
c.750-500BC	Archaic Period
c.500-336BC	Classical Period
c.336-146BC	Hellenistic Period

*c. stands for circa, which means "about".

The City of Athens

Acropolis

Agora (marketplace)

The city of Athens dates back to Mycenaean times. It was built around the *acropolis* (meaning "high town"), the city's strongest point. The Athenians claimed that they were descended from the Ionians, who had lived in Greece before the coming of the Dorians. In the Classical Period, there were probably just over a quarter of a million people in Athens and the surrounding countryside. It was a wealthy city, partly due to the possession of rich silver mines at Laureum. These helped pay for the navy and foreign trade. There was a port at Piraeus, about 6km from Athens.

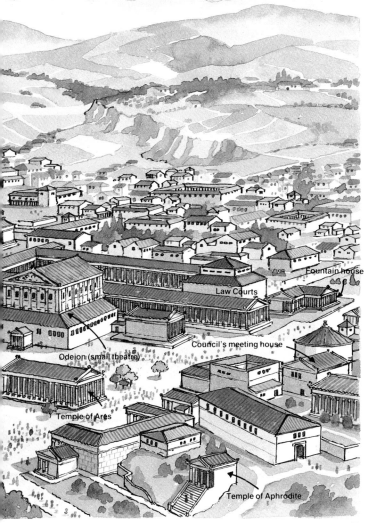

Fountain house

Law Courts

Council's meeting house

Odeion (small theatre)

Temple of Ares

Temple of Aphrodite

Houses

Part of this house has been cut away, so you can see inside.

Bedroom

Dining room

Altar

Herm

Greek houses were usually built from sun-dried mud bricks on a stone base. No complete houses have survived, but excavations give us an idea of the general layout. Houses were usually arranged around an open courtyard, which had an altar for family prayers. Many houses had an upper storey with bedrooms. The rooms at the front of the house were sometimes hired out to shopkeepers. At the front door there was a statue, called a *herm*, which was meant to guard the house.

8

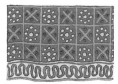

The walls inside were often plain, though lengths of patterned material may have been used as wall-hangings.

In rich people's houses the walls were sometimes painted with a patterned border. Later, whole walls were painted too.

By Hellenistic times, wealthy people had floors decorated with mosaics – pictures made from coloured stones or pebbles.

Some houses had a well in the courtyard, which meant that the house was supplied with as much water as was needed.

Most people, however, had to fetch their water from public fountains. This job was left to the women, although it involved carrying heavy jars. The public fountain was a place where women could meet each other and talk.

In Greek houses there were separate living quarters for men and women. The women spent much of their time spinning and weaving in the loom room.

In the kitchen, women ground grain into flour to make bread. There were pottery ovens for baking bread and charcoal fires for cooking meat and vegetables. The smoke escaped through a hole in the roof.

There were store rooms for keeping supplies of food, oil and wine. Wine was kept in storage jars, called *amphorae*.

Furniture

Most Greek furniture was made of wood and bronze. Although very little has survived, statues, carved stone reliefs and paintings on pots show us what it was like. Wealthy people had beautifully carved furniture, inlaid with gold, silver and ivory. Poorer people had plainer furniture.

Chairs and stools

A *thronos* was a special chair, usually made of marble. It was meant for an important official or a god.

Chairs like this one, with a back and arms, were reserved for the master of the house and honoured guests. They often had a footstool.

A *klismos* was a graceful chair with a curved back and legs. It had a seat of plaited leather and often a cushion on top.

Carvings and inlays on furniture showed designs of birds, animals, imaginary creatures, flowers and plants.

Most people sat on stools rather than chairs. A stool was called a *diphros*. Some had straight legs, others were curved. Some stools could be folded and carried.

Beds and couches

Couch

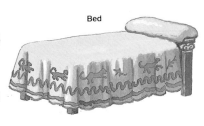
Bed

Beds and couches were both the same shape and had mattresses and pillows. Couches were used by

men for reclining on, particularly at mealtimes. Beds had covers on them as well.

Chests, boxes and baskets

There were no cupboards, so people used chests and baskets for storing clothes, documents and other things. Many women had small caskets for keeping their jewels in.

As this carved relief shows, many things were simply hung on pegs on the wall.

Tables

Tables were usually low, so that they could be tucked under couches after meals. Most tables were oblong and often only had three legs. There were round and oval tables too.

Lamps

Greek houses were lit by oil-burning lamps, made of pottery or metal. There were special stands on which the lamps could be stood or hung.

Baths and basins

Very few houses had baths, so most people used basins instead. This painting shows someone preparing for a wash.

11

Clothes

The basic article of clothing for both men and women was the *chiton*, a tunic made from a rectangular piece of cloth. Men usually wore it just above the knee and women wore it full-length.

Women's clothes

There were two main styles of women's dresses – the Doric and the Ionic. The Doric *chiton* was usually made of wool. The cloth was folded in half lengthways and folded over at the top. It was fastened at the shoulder with brooches. Sometimes the side was sewn up.

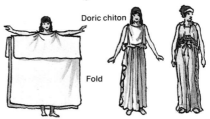

Doric chiton

Fold

The Ionic *chiton* was made of two pieces of cloth, usually linen, sewn up at the sides. It was left open at the top, but fastened together in several places. This style began being worn in Athens in the 6th century BC. Late in the Classical Period, silk and cotton were also being worn.

Ionic chiton

Dresses were sometimes worn with belts or binding across the chest.

Some materials were patterned or had patterned borders.

Cloaks and shawls

Light shawls were worn in a variety of different styles. Outdoors, women wrapped themselves in huge cloaks. They sometimes wore a hat too, to protect them from the sun.

Men's clothes

Men's tunics were made of wool or linen. They were fastened with a brooch at one or both shoulders and a belt was worn round the waist.

Although plain tunics were common, some tunics were patterned all over or had decorated borders.

Longer tunics were worn on ceremonial occasions and by older men.

Cloaks

As their climate was so warm, the Greeks did not need many clothes. A large, rectangular piece of cloth, called a *himation,* was often worn wrapped around the body, without a tunic underneath. Young men sometimes wore only a short cloak, called a *chlamys.* For travelling, cloaks were worn over tunics.

Chlamys

Himation

Hats

Travellers wore caps, or broad-brimmed hats, like these.

Shoes

Many people went barefoot most of the time. Sandals were the most common form of footwear for both men and women, although boots and shoes were worn sometimes.

13

Jewellery

Archaeologists have found some magnificent Ancient Greek jewellery. The Greeks were especially good at gold and silver work and used enamels to give a touch of colour. Until the Hellenistic Period, coloured gemstones were not widely used except in rings. Cheap jewellery was made from bronze, iron and lead.

Pins and brooches were used to fasten tunics and cloaks. Decorated metal rosettes have been found which may have been sewn on to very expensive clothes.

Rings were made entirely of metal or with a carved, coloured stone. Some were in the form of signet rings.

A lot of Greek women wore drop earrings. Some were very elaborate and detailed.

Various styles of jewelled headbands, or diadems, were worn by noblewomen. Men sometimes wore a plain headband.

Bracelets and armlets were often decorated with animal heads. Another popular design was this snake bracelet.

Women wore many styles of delicately made necklaces and chains. At first men wore very little jewellery – only brooches on their tunics, and rings – but later it became fashionable to wear more.

14

Make-up and Hairstyles

Make-up and perfume were worn by women who could afford it. They used a powder made from white lead to whiten their faces and rouge to make their cheeks pink. The eyes and lips were painted too. A mixture containing arsenic was used to remove unwanted hair from the body.

Instead of using soap the Greeks rubbed their bodies with oil. When they scraped it off, the dirt came off with it.

This painting shows a girl washing her hair. Fair hair was fashionable for a time and some women dyed their hair or wore wigs.

Mirror

Aryballoi (perfume flasks)

Alabastron (oil jar)

Comb

Pyxides (powder jars)

This mirror and the jars and flasks for cosmetics would have belonged to a wealthy Greek woman.

Hairstyles

Women grew their hair to at least shoulder length and had it arranged in curls. It was worn loose or piled on top in various different styles, and held in place by pins, ribbons and scarves. Here is a selection of styles.

Greek men had short or, at most, shoulder length hair. Most of them wore beards, though the younger ones were often clean shaven. By the Hellenistic Period, beards had started going out of fashion.

The barber's shop was a good place to go and meet friends, while you had your hair and beard trimmed.

Shopping and Money

The marketplace in a Greek city was called the *agora*. In Athens it was surrounded by important public buildings. Traders set up stalls in the open air or in the *stoa* (the colonnade). Others sold goods straight from their workshops. It was usually the men who did the shopping. The richer ones would take a slave with them to carry the purchases home. The *agora* was also a place where men went to meet their friends. Employers went to hire workmen or buy slaves.

Restaurant

Potter's shop

In Athens, officials were appointed to check the weights and measures and the quality of goods on sale.

In early times there was no money, so people bartered (exchanged goods that they agreed were of similar value).

Later, goods were exchanged for an agreed amount of metal, such as gold, silver, copper or iron.

The first coins

Coins were being made in Lydia, a Greek colony in Turkey, sometime before 600BC. Electrum (a mixture of gold and silver) was made into pieces of exactly the same weight and purity. They were stamped by the government to certify this. Later, other Greek cities adopted their own coinage.

When you visited another city, you had to go to a moneychanger who, for a fee, would change your coins for you.

Later, banks were set up. Bankers lent their own and their clients' money to customers, who had to repay the money with interest.

Coins

Greek coins were made of gold or silver. At first each coin was stamped with the symbol of its city. Later gods and goddesses were shown, and later still, portraits of rulers. The most common Greek coin was the *drachma*. In Athens there were six *obols* to one *drachma*, two *drachmae** to one *stater*, 50 *staters* to one *mina*, and 60 *minae* to one *talent*. Here is a selection of coins from different cities.

Early electrum coin from Lydia, from the reign of King Croesus (c. 561-546BC)

Early gold coin with writing on it. Origin unknown.

Coin from Corinth, showing Pegasus, the winged horse.

Coin from Peparethus. c. 500BC.

Coin from Syracuse, showing the head of the nymph, Arethusa c. 415BC.

Coin from Athens, with an owl, the symbol of Athens. c. 500BC.

Coin from Syracuse, showing Arethusa and some dolphins. c. 479BC.

Coin from Macedon, showing King Philip of Macedon. c. 360-338BC.

*The plural of drachma.   *c. stands for circa, which means "about".

17

Family Life

When a baby was born, the mother presented it to the father. If he refused to accept it, it was put out to die.

Once the baby was accepted, celebrations were held to present it to the gods and give it a name.

In wealthy families the child was put into the care of a nurse, who often looked after it until it grew up.

The Greeks had some furniture made specially for babies. This cot on wheels was shown in a painting.

This is a high chair. Some chairs had a potty placed in the lower part of the stand.

This baby's feeding bottle and rattle in the shape of a pig were found on the sites of Ancient Greek houses.

Toys and games

Up to the age of seven, Greek children had nothing to do but play. Here are some of their toys and the games they played.

Ball games

Doll

Toy goose and rider

Rolling hoops

Riding in a cart

Yo-yo

Playing on swings

18

At 18, a boy officially came of age. There were celebrations and garlands of flowers were hung on the doors.

When a girl was about 15, her father chose a husband for her. The groom was often much older, as many Greek men delayed marrying for a long time. Here the bride is being dressed and prepared for the ceremony.

Wedding celebrations began at the bride's home with a sacrifice at the altar. The bride was crowned and presented to the groom by her father. Then she was led to her new home in a procession led by musicians and a torch bearer.

The groom carried the bride over the threshold. Then they made an offering to the gods and shared a special cake together.

Women's lives

Greek women were always under the control of their nearest male relative – their father, husband or son. Husbands were paid a dowry – a gift of money or property – by their father-in-law. This had to be returned if there was a divorce. Men could divorce their wives by sending them away, but women had to act through an official.

Women from wealthy families spent most of their time at home, in the women's quarters. They had to make sure the store rooms were well stocked and the house was clean. They supervised the slave women preparing wool, spinning and weaving.

There was very little opportunity to get out of the house. A rich woman who wanted to do some shopping had to be escorted by a slave.

This did not apply to ordinary women, who had no slaves. They had more freedom as they had to do many things for themselves.

Education

Boys went to school between the ages of seven and 15. All citizens were expected to send their sons to school, but as fees were charged, poor boys probably did not stay very long. A boy from a wealthy family was taken to school by a slave called a *pedagogue,* who would stay during the lessons, possibly helping to keep order in the classroom. Schools taught reading, writing and sums, music, poetry, sport and gymnastics.

Girls were taught at home by their mothers. They learnt the skills needed to run a home, such as cooking, spinning and weaving.

Schoolchildren wrote with a stylus on a wooden tablet covered with wax. You could rub out the mistakes and re-use the tablet.

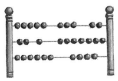

Sums were worked out on a frame called an abacus. The beads were worth one each on the top row, 10 each on the second row and 100 each on the third.

Children read the works of great authors and poets, such as Homer and learnt poetry by heart.

In music lessons they were taught to sing and dance and to play the lyre and the pipes.

Athletics played an important part in a boy's education, especially after the age of 14.

At 18 a boy was a full citizen. He then became an *ephebe,* which meant doing two years military service.

Although there were no universities, men like the philosopher Plato set up schools of further education.

Teachers called sophists taught young men how to present arguments.

Education in Sparta

In Sparta all children belonged to the state. A committee of elders decided if a baby was healthy enough to be allowed to live. At seven, boys were taken away from home and sent to a kind of boarding school, called a *pedonome,* where the discipline was very strict.

A Spartan education aimed to make children tough. The boys were given only one tunic a year to wear. They had no sandals and no bedclothes and they had to sleep on the ground.

They were kept hungry, so they had to steal for food. This was supposed to teach them stealth and cunning and to train them to live off enemy land when they became soldiers.

Most of their training was concerned with making them into good soldiers. They spent a lot of time learning how to use weapons and very little on academic work.

The boys were savagely beaten to teach them courage. There were competitions to see who could suffer most without complaining.

They learnt songs about war and love for their country. Dancing lessons were supposed to make them strong and agile.

The Spartans valued the wisdom of old people. Young Spartans were taught to show respect at all times.

Boys were allowed to attend public dinners, which were held once a month, to enable them to learn from the conversation of the men.

Although Spartan girls did not go to school, they were also brought up to be tough. Their education included wrestling and athletics.

Games, Music and Entertainment

Greek men went regularly to the town sports centre – the *gymnasium* – for exercise, such as wrestling, and to meet friends and talk.

They also played energetic ball games. This carving shows a game which looks rather like hockey.

Setting two cocks to fight to the death was regarded as an exciting sport. Sometimes other animals were used.

The Greeks had board games too. The two soldiers in this vase painting are playing a game that may have been something like draughts.

Knucklebones was a game played with four bones, which you tossed in the air. The sides of the bones were numbered and you needed a certain combination of numbers to win.

Music and dancing

Although music played an important part in Greek education, most professional musicians and dancers were slaves or freed slaves. They were trained at special schools. Some became attached to a family and entertained guests at dinner. Others could be hired for parties and special occasions.

Pan-pipes

Lyre

Pipes

Kithara

Cymbals

Tambourine

Some religious festivals provided an opportunity for ordinary citizens to dance.

Here is a selection of Greek musical instruments. The pan-pipes were named after the god Pan, who was said to have invented them.

Parties

Greek dinner parties were for men only, although some clever and beautiful unmarried women, called *hetairai,* might be invited too. The guests sat around on couches in the *andron* (the dining room), each with his own table. Slaves served the food and presented the guests with wreaths of flowers to wear. After the meal, the men stayed to drink and have a discussion, called a *symposium.*

The Greeks always drank their wine mixed with water. The wine was mixed in a huge jar, called a *krater.*

People ate their food with their fingers. Slaves stood by to wash the guests' fingers between courses.

Cottabos was a popular game played at dinner. You kept some wine in your cup and flicked it at a chosen target.

A whole range of entertainers could be hired for parties. There were jugglers, acrobats, sword dancers, comedians, story tellers and actors as well as dancers accompanied by musicians.

The Olympic Games

The Olympic Games were held once every four years at Olympia, in honour of Zeus, king of the gods. There were other festivals which held sporting events, but these were the most famous. Men came from all over Greece and the colonies to watch them. All wars were postponed for three months to allow people to travel in safety. The Olympic Games probably date back to 776BC.

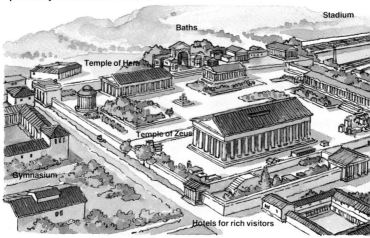

Stadium

Baths

Temple of Hera

Temple of Zeus

Gymnasium

Hotels for rich visitors

There were temples and altars where people came to worship the gods and make sacrifices. This statue of Zeus, which stood in his temple at Olympia, was 13m high and made of gold and ivory.

The athletes covered their bodies with oil, as a protection against sun and dirt. After the contest, it was scraped off with a curved instrument, called a *strigil*.

Judges watched all the events from a special stand in the stadium. Many of the other spectators had to stand as there were few seats.

The winners were given ribbons, palm branches or wreaths as prizes. They competed for glory, rather than money. At the end of the games there was a huge banquet.

24

The contests

The Olympic Games lasted for five days. All the athletes were men. One of the contests, the *pentathlon,* was for all-round athletes. This involved taking part in five events – discus, javelin, jumping, running and wrestling – all in one afternoon.

The oldest event was running. The races were either one, two or 24 lengths of the stadium.

In one race the men wore helmets and greaves (leg guards) and carried shields.

Another event was discus-throwing. The discus was a flat, bronze disc, about the size of a dinner plate.

Javelin throwers wound a leather thong round their fingers. This helped them to throw the javelin more smoothly.

Long jumpers carried weights, which they swung forward as they jumped.

Chariot races were included in the games. At one time there were races for chariots drawn by mules.

Horse races and chariot races were held in the *hippodrome**. The jockeys raced without saddles or stirrups.

In wrestling, either the contest went on till one man gave up, or the victor had to throw his opponent three times.

The *pankration* was a violent form of fighting. But there were strict rules and referees kept a look out for fouls.

Boxers wore leather thongs wound round their hands, sometimes with a piece of sheepskin underneath.

There were separate games in which women could take part. These were part of a festival for the goddess Hera.

*Hippo *is the Greek for horse.*

The Theatre

Drama developed from the songs and dances performed in Athens at the festival of Dionysus, the god of wine. The songs in the god's honour were sung by a group of 12 to 15 men, called the chorus. Then an actor was included, who talked with the leader of the chorus. As more actors took part, the words and action became more important and proper plays were written.

Skene (stage)

Chorus

Orchestra

Plays were performed in theatres in the open air. Seats for the audience were cut into the slope of a hillside. They were made of wood at first, but were later replaced by stone. The philosopher Plato tells us that in some theatres there was room for up to 30,000 people. Performances lasted all day, with several plays in a row.

These bronze tickets told you which block of seats to sit in. They cost two *obols* each. Poor people could get help from public funds to pay for them.

Important people, such as judges and local officials sat in the front. This seat of honour was for the priest of Dionysus.

Plays were divided into tragedies and comedies. The judges awarded ivy wreaths to the authors of the best tragedy and the best comedy.

Tragedies

Tragedies told sad tales about the conflicts of love, honour and religious duty. They were usually based on stories the audience knew well, such as the Trojan War. This painting shows Queen Clytemnestra killing the Trojan princess, Cassandra.

The chorus sometimes sang and danced, but their main role was making speeches to tell you more about the story.

Comedies

This painting shows a scene from a comedy. Comedies made fun of all kinds of things, including politics, religion and important local personalities.

In comedies the chorus sometimes represented animals. This painting shows them dressed as birds.

Costumes

All the actors wore masks, with different facial expressions. They changed masks to show the changes in mood of the character. Wide mouths in the masks helped them project their voices.

In comedies the actors wore padded clothes to make them look funnier. There were no female actors, so men had to dress as women to play the women's parts.

Scenery

The scenery was usually painted to look like a palace or temple, as shown on this piece of painted pot.

Scene changes were rare. They were probably done by revolving part of the wall, like this.

Farming

Many people in Ancient Greece were farmers. Good farming land was scarce though, as much of the country is mountainous and the soil poor. The main crops were wheat, barley, grapes and olives. The best grazing land was in the marshy regions of Thessaly and Boeotia. Elsewhere there was very little good pasture, so only a few farms were able to keep horses or cattle for meat. Most farmers only had oxen for ploughing the fields.

Wheat and barley were grown on the plains. A farmer's year began in October. He ploughed the land, while someone behind him sowed the grain by hand. Every year some of the land was left fallow (not planted), so that the soil could regain its goodness.

The crops grew during the winter when there was rain. In May it was ready to be harvested with sickles.

To thresh the grain, or separate it from the straw, animals were driven over it on paved circular floors. Then it was winnowed (separated from the chaff, or husks). This was done by throwing the grain up into the air, so that the light chaff blew away.

Grapes were grown in vineyards on the lower hill slopes. They were picked in September.

Some grapes were kept for eating and the rest were made into wine. Men trod the grapes with their feet to get the juice out. It was then poured into jars and left to ferment into wine.

To pick olives, men climbed the trees or knocked the olives down with poles. The trees were protected by law and could not be uprooted.

To extract the oil, the olives were crushed in a press, like this. Olive oil was used for cooking, lighting and cleaning the body.

Farmers also grew vegetables. These included peas, beans, turnips, cucumbers, garlic, onions, lettuces, leeks, artichokes, carrots and pumpkins. Fruit and nuts, such as apples, pears, plums, figs, almonds, pomegranates and melons were also grown.

A few wealthy farmers had horses for riding or pulling chariots.

Sheep and goats grazed on the hillsides. Goats supplied meat, milk and cheese. Sheep were kept for wool and some meat.

Farmers also kept pigs and poultry for meat and eggs.

Hunting wild animals, such as deer, hares and wild boars, was a way of supplementing the food produced on farms.

What the Greeks ate

Most people in Ancient Greece lived mainly on a kind of porridge, bread, cheese, fruit, vegetables and eggs. Meat was a rare treat, unless you were rich. Breakfast and lunch were both fairly light meals. The main meal was in the evening.

As most Greeks lived near the sea, fish, eaten fresh or dried, was an important source of protein.

They used honey to sweeten their food, as they had no sugar. Bees were kept in pottery hives.

People's Jobs

Many Greeks earned their living as craftsmen. The skills were probably passed down from father to son, or through another member of the family. Most workshops were small. They were run by a family with their slaves – probably six men in all, though there were some large businesses using a lot of slaves. Some men kept slaves specially for hiring out to employers in need of extra workmen. Greek women worked in the home.

Carpenters made furniture, parts of weapons and tools and were employed in building work. These men are finishing off a chest.

Pottery

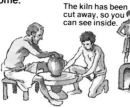

The kiln has been cut away, so you can see inside. Air vent

Pottery was an important craft as potters made many household goods, such as lamps and cooking pots. First they dug clay and mixed it with water. One potter shaped the pot while his assistant turned the wheel. Then the pot was fired (baked) in a kiln.

Painting pots

The Greek art of painting pottery was admired all over the Ancient World. First the design was painted on the unfired pot with a mixture of clay, water and probably wood ash. The pot was put in the kiln to begin the firing process. Then all the openings in the kiln were closed. The lack of air made the pot turn black. Air was then allowed in again. The painted parts stayed black and the rest of the pot turned red. This process might have taken years to get right.

Mining

This man is working in a silver mine. Mines and quarries were owned by the state and leased to private citizens. They employed a lot of slaves, often in very bad conditions.

Iron working

Iron was used mainly for tools and weapons. Iron ore was mixed with charcoal and put into a furnace. Lumps of metal formed at the bottom, which were reheated before being hammered into shape.

Bronze working

The Greeks were experts at the "lost wax" method of bronze working. First a clay core was made and pins stuck in it. The statue was modelled round the core in wax and then the whole thing was covered with clay. The clay-covered model was heated, which made the wax melt and run out. The core was still held in place by the pins.

Molten bronze was poured in where the wax had been. When the bronze had set, the clay mould was removed.

There were other methods of working bronze. It could be poured straight into ordinary moulds (right) or heated a little, to make it soften, and then hammered into shape (left).

Sculpture

Here is a sculptor at work carving a *herm*, a statue of a god which people stood at their front doors. Sculptors made statues of stone, bronze, wood, ivory and gold.

Finishing off a stone statue involved painting it. Greek statues were always painted, either all over or in parts. The paint has since worn away, leaving the bare stone.

Here is a cobbler at work. Some skilled slaves were set up in business by their masters, in return for a share of the profits.

Skilled boat-builders were always in demand to supply boats for fishing, for the navy and for travelling.

Some men worked as part-time fishermen, in order to provide their families with extra food.

Pottery

Greek pots and vases were painted by skilled artists, but they were also strong and practical. They were not treated as ornaments, but were made only for daily use. Here is a guide to help you recognize the main shapes and styles.

Recognizing styles

Pots with **geometric** patterns, like this, date from 900–700BC.

The **protogeometric** style dates from 1000 to 900BC. Look out for circles or semi-circles on the design.

The 6th century BC was the period of the **orientalizing style**, ▶ influenced by the East. The decoration includes animals and plants.

Black figure ware – black figures on a reddish background – was produced between 600 and 530BC.

Red figure ware – red figures on a black background – dates from 530BC.

Figures painted on a white background are found on vases dating from 500BC.

Some potters made cups in the form of animal or human heads.

From about 400BC, the standard of pottery declined. Pots either imitated metal vases (above), or were fussy and over-decorated.

Recognizing shapes

Amphorae were used for storing wine. They are one of the most common types of pot.

A *stamnos* (left) and a *pelike* (right) were also storage jars.

The Greeks drank wine mixed with water, which was served from a jug. The one on the left is an *olpe,* the one on the right, an *oinochoe.*

Some cups were large, so that they could be passed round all the guests at a ceremony. The handles were designed so that people lying on couches could hold them easily.

Greek women carried water in a jar, called a *hydria.* It was specially designed with three handles.

Kraters were bowls for mixing wine and water. The one on the left is called a *volute krater.*

A *kyathos* was a ladle. It was used for serving wine from a *krater* into cups and jugs.

Oils and perfumes were kept in small bottles, like these – an *aryballos* (left), an *alabastron* (centre) and a *lekythos* (right). The pot on the far right is a *pyxis,* used for storing cosmetics.

Gods and Goddesses

The Greeks believed in many gods and had hundreds of stories about them. There were local gods and gods to look after all aspects of life and death. According to legend, Mother Earth gave birth to all living things. The first gods were called the Titans. Zeus, the son of two Titans called Chronos and Rhea, seized power for himself and his brothers and sisters. In Classical times they were the most important gods. They were called Olympians, as they were said to live on Mount Olympus.

Zeus, god of the sky and thunder, ruled the gods on Mount Olympus. **Hera,** his wife and sister, was goddess of all women.

Demeter, a sister of Zeus, was goddess of the earth and corn.

Aphrodite was goddess of love and beauty. Her son, **Eros,** made people fall in love by shooting them with arrows. **Hephaestos,** her husband, was the gods' craftsman.

Ares was god of war. He loved Aphrodite.

Athene, daughter of Zeus, was goddess of wisdom and Athens. Her symbol was an owl.

Apollo was god of the sun and patron of music, poetry and healing.

Artemis was goddess of the moon, hunting and women.

Poseidon, brother of Zeus, was god of the sea.

Hermes was messenger of the gods and patron of merchants and travellers. He took the dead to the Underworld.

Pluto, Zeus's brother, ruled the Underworld, the world of the dead. Demeter's daughter, **Persephone,** whom he had kidnapped, ruled with him. Demeter's grief over this caused winter, but every year Persephone returned to her mother and so brought the spring. ▶

Dionysus was god of wine.

Pan, god of the countryside, was half-goat. He played the pan-pipes.

Asclepius, son of Apollo, was god of medicine. His symbol was snakes.

Lesser gods and spirits

Beneath the great gods and goddesses was a host of divine beings. Here are some of them.

Centaurs were half-men, half-horses.

Nine **muses** looked after music and learning.

Nymphs were beautiful girls who lived in trees and streams.

The **Furies,** were dog-headed, bat-winged creatures, with snakes for hair. They pursued murderers and drove them mad.

Boreas was the north wind.

Charon ferried the dead across the River Styx to the Underworld. **Cerberus** was a three-headed god, who guarded the entrance.

35

Heroes

Many Greek poems and plays are based on the stories of their legendary heroes. Some of them had probably been real people in Mycenaean times, or earlier. As time passed, the stories were changed and added to, until they became full of supernatural deeds. Here are a few of the main characters.

Herakles was given 12 impossible tasks, which included fighting terrible monsters. He succeeded and became a god.

Theseus killed the Minotaur, a monster which lived in Crete, in an underground maze, or labyrinth, and ate humans.

There were many stories about the Trojan War. This was caused by the elopement of Paris, a prince of Troy, with Queen Helen of Sparta.

The Greeks went to Troy to try to get her back. After a ten year siege, the Trojans were defeated. The Greeks tricked them by hiding soldiers inside a wooden horse, which they presented to the Trojans as a gift.

The Odyssey tells of the hero, Odysseus, and of the many things that happened to him on his way back from the Trojan War.

Jason and his companions, the Argonauts, sailed in search of the Golden Fleece. They won it with the help of Princess Medea.

Jason married Medea, but then deserted her. In revenge, she killed their children and escaped in a chariot drawn by dragons.

Oedipus, ignorant of his real identity, killed his father and married his mother. This enraged the gods and brought disaster.

Perseus wore winged sandals that enabled him to fly. He killed the Gorgon Medusa and rescued a princess from a sea monster.

Bellerophon tamed the winged horse, Pegasus, and so was able to kill the lion-headed, serpent-tailed, fire-breathing Chimera.

Religion

Greek houses had altars for family worship. People burnt incense there, made offerings of food and said prayers to the god or goddess they felt could help them best.

A temple was the home of a god or goddess. This is a model of an early temple, which would have been made of brick or wood. It had a chamber, called a *cella* and a columned porch.

As time passed, larger, more elaborate temples were built of stone, with tiled or stone roofs. This is the temple of the Parthenon in Athens, dedicated to the worship of the goddess, Athene.

A statue of the god or goddess stood in the *cella*. Inside the Parthenon was a 12m high statue of Athene, made of gold and ivory. People visited the temple to pray privately, but there were no services inside for a congregation.

The temple treasury contained offerings, such as jewellery, given by people who wanted to win favour with the gods or thank them.

Priests and priestesses were appointed to perform daily rituals in the service of the god or goddess, such as burning incense or presenting food offerings. A few temples had special priestesses who were young girls.

Festivals

The Greeks had many festivals to celebrate the feast days of their gods and goddesses. An animal was sacrificed at a special altar outside the temple. The sex, colour and type of animal was different for each god. There were hymns and prayers, and incense was burned. When praying to an Underworld god, you held the palms of your hands downwards. For the other gods, the palms faced upwards. There were usually processions and often theatrical and athletic competitions too.

The most important festival in Athens was the Great Panathenia, the feast of the goddess Athene. A procession led to the Parthenon, taking a beautiful new robe to Athene. It was held every four years, with a less splendid festival on the years in between.

People often sang and danced in the processions. The festivals in honour of Dionysus often became very wild. The worshippers were drunk with wine, and were known to kill animals, and even people, until efforts were made to control them.

In the Anthesteria festival of Dionysus at Athens, three year old children took part and were given tiny jugs, like these, as presents.

Mystery cults

A mystery cult was a secret cult associated with a particular god or goddess. The most famous was that of Demeter and Persephone at Eleusis. You joined in stages and learned a new secret at each stage. The members never revealed the secrets, so we know very little about them.

This scene shows what may have happened at the final initiation ceremony at Eleusis. The new member is received into the cult by the goddesses themselves, who were priestesses acting the parts.

Messages from the gods

The Greeks believed that priests called soothsayers could interpret messages from the gods. They thought that things such as thunderstorms, dreams and the birth of a deformed animal were messages from the gods.

By watching the flight of birds or examining the insides of a sacrificed animal, they could find out if the gods favoured something.

Oracles

If you wanted a direct answer from a god to a difficult problem, you could ask an oracle. The most famous was the oracle of Apollo at Delphi. You sent the god a written question. Then a priestess, called the Pythia, went into a trance and spoke for the god. A priest interpreted her often confused replies.

Funerals and the Underworld

A dead person was dressed in white and laid in state in the house, so friends and relatives could pay their last respects.

The next day the body was taken to the tomb – in a carriage if the family were wealthy. A procession followed with music and professional women mourners. The body, or its burnt ashes, was then placed in the tomb, with offerings of food and personal possessions.

People went on making regular offerings to their dead relatives long after the funeral.

The Greeks believed dead people went to the Underworld, a grey, shadowy kingdom where ordinary people just roamed around. The wicked were given punishments, but the very good were granted eternal happiness in the Elysian Fields.

Greek Armies

In the Classical Period each city state had its own army. All citizens were expected to fight whenever they were needed. There was almost always a war going on somewhere in Greece. When one city wanted to fight another, an animal was sacrificed and its insides were examined, to see if the gods were in favour of a war. Then a herald was sent to declare war. The Athenian army was commanded by ten generals.

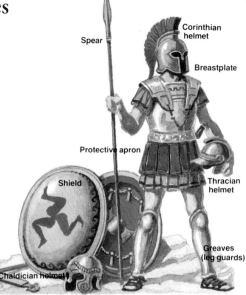

Spear

Corinthian helmet

Breastplate

Protective apron

Shield

Thracian helmet

Sword

Greaves (leg guards)

Chaldician helmet

Here is a selection of the armour and weapons that were used. Each soldier had to provide his own. Poor citizens, who could not afford to buy armour, usually joined the navy and became rowers instead.

Greek men were taught how to fight when they were at school. In battle, they fought shoulder to shoulder in a formation called a phalanx. They usually threw their spears and then charged at the enemy to try to break their ranks.

Thessaly and Boeotia had cavalry, but most armies used mounted soldiers only as scouts.

The Spartan army

Spartan soldiers were the most feared of all the Greeks. Their education system was specially designed to produce good, obedient soldiers. Even after they married, at the age of 30, they continued to live in the military barracks. The Spartan army was commanded by one of the two Spartan kings*.

Each army usually had a small force of archers and another of lightly-armed javelin throwers.

This vase painting shows a wounded soldier being bandaged.

40 *See page 49.

In the Hellenistic Period, cavalry played a more important role. Philip of Macedon and his son, Alexander, were both brilliant commanders, who used infantry and cavalry together.

They favoured lighter armour, so that the soldiers could move more quickly. Much longer pikes were used, up to 6m in length.

Siege warfare

A tactic often used was to destroy the enemy's crops. The army then tried to surround the city by land and sea, to cut off new supplies.

The historian, Thucydides, described a flame-thrower used in a seige. Huge bellows blasted air down a tube into a cauldron of burning tar. Flames from the cauldron were blown forward and spread all around.

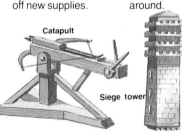

Catapult

Siege tower

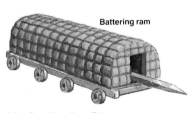

Battering ram

By about 400BC, the Greeks had started using battering rams to attack enemy walls and catapults

which fired javelins. Siege towers were used to enable soldiers to climb on to enemy walls.

Sea battles

Battles were often fought at sea. Tactics included ramming enemy ships and manoeuvring to break

their oars. Once close to an enemy ship, the soldiers would try to board it and fight.

41

Travel

At night, people took flaming torches with them, as there was no street lighting.

Most people in Greece went everywhere on foot. On longer journeys they might take a walking stick and a folding stool, so that they could rest along the way. The wealthy travelled on horseback or in horse-drawn chariots.

Bandits and the frequent wars between states made travelling in some parts of the country very dangerous.

Only a few busy routes had reasonable roads and there were hardly any bridges. In winter, carts and chariots often got stuck in the mud. For transporting goods it was easier to use donkeys or mules.

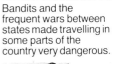

Although there were some wayside inns, they did not always offer food. People considered it a duty to offer hospitality to any traveller in need of shelter.

Sea travel

Where possible long journeys were made by sea, instead of overland. The best time for sailing was in the summer. Sea travel had its dangers

too – from storms, rocky coasts and pirates. Many wrecks have been found by underwater archaeologists.

The Navy

Of all the city states, Athens had the most powerful navy. It was financed by a rich vein of silver discovered in their silver mines at Laureum in 483BC. With their fleet they were able to win many vital sea battles against their great enemies, the Persians, and to prevent an attempted invasion. Positions such as captain or helmsman were held by trained sailors, but ordinary men were employed as rowers.

Among the earliest warships were the *penteconters*. These were long ships with 50 oarsmen.

Later, the Greeks started using two banks of oarsmen on each side of the ship to give it greater speed and

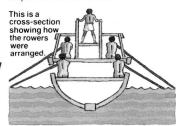

This is a cross-section showing how the rowers were arranged.

make it easier to manoeuvre. This kind of ship was called a *bireme*.

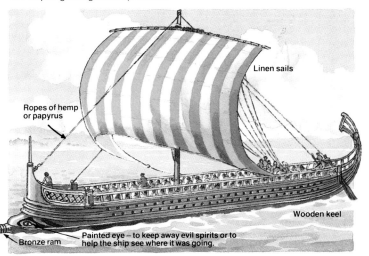

Linen sails

Ropes of hemp or papyrus

Wooden keel

Bronze ram

Painted eye – to keep away evil spirits or to help the ship see where it was going.

A *trireme* had three banks of oars, and 170 rowers, though experts differ as to how it was arranged. There was an upper deck for the soldiers to fight on. Ships went to sea for short periods only, as there was little space for cooking and sleeping. Later, *quadriremes* and *quinqueremes*, with four and five banks of oars, were built.

Trade and the Colonies

The Greek city states sold their surplus goods by trading with each other and with other lands around the Mediterranean and Black Seas. There were no large trading companies. Each merchant usually had his own ship. Some traders were rich enough to finance their own deals, but many had to borrow from bankers. In Athens, many of the richest traders were *metics* (foreigners). They were forbidden by law to own land, so many invested in trade instead.

The goods were usually sent in sturdy sailing ships, like these. To navigate, they used the stars and well-known landmarks.

Goods to be delivered inland were sent across country on the backs of mules.

Here are two traders from different parts of Greece negotiating a deal. Payment was in coins.

The main exports from Greece were wine, olive oil and manufactured goods, such as cloth, pots and statues.

Imports included grain from the Black Sea, copper, tin, timber and goods from Africa and the East, such as ivory, incense, spices, perfume, silk and slaves.

The Greeks travelled far in search of trade. This scene, based on a vase painting, shows a trader supervising the loading of a cargo at Cyrene in North Africa.

Explorers

In 300 BC, Pytheas of Massilia (Marseilles) explored northern Europe. He claimed to have sailed round the British Isles, but few believed his account of his trip.

In 120BC, a trader called Eudoxus met a shipwrecked Indian sailor who showed him how to use the monsoon winds. This enabled him to sail to India and back.

The colonies

At the time of the Dorian invasions, many people left Greece and set up colonies in Ionia, on the west coast of what is now Turkey. The next wave of colonization began in the 8th century BC. A rise in population had led to a serious shortage of farming land and many left to seek their fortunes abroad.

Families of emigrants set off with animals and supplies of food and seed for planting. They settled in largely uninhabited areas and built new cities, modelled on the Greek ones.

A map of Greek settlements

This map shows the extent of Greek settlements. The new cities provided raw materials and markets for Greek goods. They were completely independent, though fellow Greeks sometimes came to their aid when they were threatened by enemies. A tribe called the Graii settled in Italy. The Romans later called them Graeci. This word came to be used for all who spoke their language, and from it comes our word "Greek".

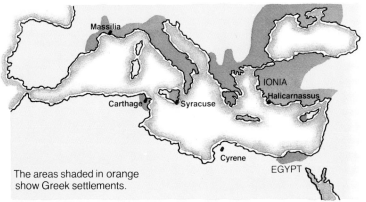

The areas shaded in orange show Greek settlements.

The Government

How city states grew up

Rulers in Mycenaean times often built their palaces in high places which could be defended easily. People settled inside the walls.

These settlements grew into towns and then cities, spreading beyond the original walls. New walls were built to enclose them.

By Classical times, Greece was divided into many small city states, each consisting of a city and the countryside and villages around it.

Types of government

In Mycenaean times, the states of Greece were ruled by kings, assisted by their nobles.

By about 800BC, most kings were replaced by oligarchies, small groups of aristocrats (from *aristoi*, meaning best people).

Many people felt their needs were ignored by the oligarchs, so they helped tyrants* to gain power. Some tyrants were good rulers, but others were cruel and unjust.

By the beginning of the Classical Period, tyrants were being replaced by democracies. In a democracy, all citizens have a say in the government. In Ancient Greece, only men could be citizens. The states were small, so most men were able to attend meetings and were encouraged to take an active part in politics. The word politics comes from the Greek word *polis*, meaning city.

In Athens, an assembly was held three or four times a month. All citizens could attend, speak and vote on government policies.

Policies to be submitted to the assembly were decided on by the council, a group of 500 men. For political purposes, the citizens of Athens were divided into ten tribes. The council contained 50 men from each tribe. Each tribe took it in turn to lead the council. Councillors served for a year.

*Tyrants were men who ruled single-handed.

At first nine men called *archons* were the chief officials. Later, they were replaced in importance by ten generals, called *strategoi,* who were elected each year by the assembly.

There was a host of lesser officials to see to the day to day running of government. They were chosen by lot, which meant that even poor citizens had the chance of becoming officials.

Poor citizens were paid a day's wage to attend the assembly. This was to enable them to take an active part in government.

Wealthy citizens were expected to make extra contributions to the state, such as paying for warships, or a new play at the theatre.

This is Perikles, a popular politician who was re-elected in Athens every year between 460 and 430BC.

To keep check on officials, there was a system called ostracism. Citizens wrote the names of officials they disapproved of on *ostraca*, pieces of broken pottery.

If a certain number of people voted against an official in this way, he was banished from Athens for ten years.

Non-citizens

There were several categories of Athenians who were not citizens. These were women, *metics* (foreigners living permanently in Athens), slaves and freed slaves. If a citizen married a foreigner, his sons could not become citizens.

Household slaves could buy their freedom by saving tips they had earned. Some were granted freedom as part of their master's will.

Slaves who were hired out for work by their masters were paid one-sixth of the wages they earned.

47

Law

In Athens most law cases were tried by juries of over 200 men who were chosen by lot. People volunteered to be jurors. Their names were written on tickets and put into the slots of an "allotment" machine (right). Coloured balls were dropped into the machine, to determine which names would be chosen.

Poor citizens who came forward as jurors were given a day's pay, to enable them to take their turn in court.

There were no lawyers, so citizens had to conduct their own cases in court. Some sought the help of professional speech-writers.

Foreigners were not allowed to speak in court, so they had to get a citizen to act for them.

To avoid long speeches, a water clock was used to limit the time allowed to each speaker. The jar was filled with water to just below the rim and the water dripped out through a hole in the bottom.

The jurors gave their verdicts on the case with ballot discs. The discs with solid knobs meant "innocent", the ones with hollow knobs meant "guilty".

A different system was used for trials involving murder or treason. Treason trials were heard and judged by the whole assembly. Cases of murder were judged by officials in a special court.

The Athenian Law against Tyranny of 336BC is recorded on this tablet. It states that there is no punishment for murdering a tyrant (someone who tries to overthrow democracy and seize power for himself).

Government and Society in Sparta

In about 600BC, the Spartan ruling classes began to cut themselves off from other states and dedicated themselves to war against rival states and rebellious subjects. Spartan citizens (who were all men) became full-time soldiers, living permanently in barracks.

At the age of 30, they were divided by election into "equals" and "inferiors". Only equals had full political rights and could attend the assembly. At the assembly, people voted for or against proposals by shouting.

The proposals to be put to the assembly were decided by a council of elders, a group of men over 60, who were elected by the assembly.

Above the council were five officials, called *ephors*, who were elected each year to run the government.

They were also two Spartan kings, who acted as both military and religious leaders.

The Spartan territory was made up of the provinces of Laconia and Messenia. They had one valuable natural resource – iron.

All the jobs in trade and industry were done by Spartan subjects, called *periokoi*. They were not citizens, but were allowed some say in local affairs and could serve in the army. This left the citizens free to devote themselves to war.

All farming work was done by the helots, descendants of the people who had lived in Sparta before the invasion of the Dorians*. The helots were little more than slaves, producing food for the Spartans.

Many helots were discontented and tried to rebel against their rulers, but the rebellions were always crushed.

*The Spartan rulers were descendants of the Dorians.

Architecture

Architectural styles in many parts of the world have been based on those of the Ancient Greeks. The Greeks used their knowledge of mathematics to produce buildings with beautiful proportions. At first the materials used were sun-dried bricks and wood, but these were replaced by limestone and, later, marble.

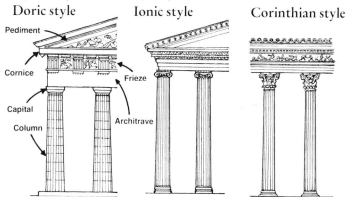

Doric style

- Pediment
- Cornice
- Frieze
- Capital
- Architrave
- Column

Ionic style

Corinthian style

Greek architecture is divided into two main styles – the Doric and the Ionic. A later style, the Corinthian, developed from the Ionic. You can recognize these styles from the types of columns used. This picture shows the names of the different parts of the front of a temple.

Sometimes a *caryatid*, a figure of a girl, took the place of an ordinary column. ▶ The most famous are in the Erechtheion in Athens.

A circular building was called a *tholos*. Most were used as religious shrines, but there was one in Athens which was used for council meetings.

◀ This eight-sided building is the Tower of the Winds in Athens, which is still intact. It was built to house a huge water clock.

A colonnade like this was called a *stoa*. These were built round markets and other places, to protect people from the sun and rain.

Monuments

Monuments of various kinds were built to honour people and great events.

These are monuments marking graves.

The lion of Chaeronea marks the site of an important battle won by King Philip of Macedon.

Lysicrates built this to commemorate a prize he had won in the theatre.

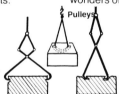

The great altar at Pergamon was erected in the first century BC. The carvings on it tell the tale of a war between gods and giants.

The tomb of King Mausolus (from whom we get the word mausoleum) was so magnificent that it once counted as one of the seven wonders of the world.

Building methods

Public buildings were made from blocks of stone cut from quarries. Teams of workmen hauled the blocks into place. From Greek authors we know that pulleys were also used to lift blocks, but no picture or actual pulley has survived.

Pulleys

Grooves cut into blocks of stone give us an idea of how they were gripped by the pulleys.

Instead of using cement, the Greeks joined blocks of stone together with bronze or iron cramps, like these.

Columns were held together with wooden pegs placed in the top and bottom of each section.

Town planning ▶

By the Classical Period, new Greek cities were being planned on a grid system. The streets were laid out in rows which crossed at right angles.

Sculpture and Craftwork

Greek sculptors made statues and carvings for temples, tombs and monuments. The most common subjects were gods, goddesses and heroes. Statues were made from a variety of materials, including marble, limestone, bronze, wood, terracotta, ivory and gold. Most of the surviving statues were made of stone. Many bronze statues were melted down and the metal reused.

Archaic Period

Statues from the Archaic Period look stiff and formal. They were based on Egyptian and eastern styles. The statues are of three main types: the seated figure, the *kouros* (standing youth) and the *kore* (standing girl).

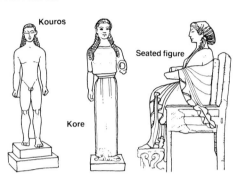

Kouros

Kore

Seated figure

Classical Period

By Classical times, the Greeks had learned how to portray the human body in a completely life-like way. Skilled portraits of important people began to be made as well as sculptures showing scenes and actions. Faces in the scenes often showed expression and emotion, although the ones in portraits were always calm and composed.

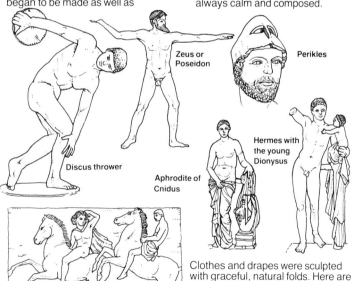

Discus thrower

Zeus or Poseidon

Perikles

Aphrodite of Cnidus

Hermes with the young Dionysus

Clothes and drapes were sculpted with graceful, natural folds. Here are two statues (one a Roman copy, the other probably an original) by the famous Greek sculptor, Praxiteles.

Hellenistic Period

By the Hellenistic Period, a much wider range of subjects was chosen. Outstanding portraits were produced and children, foreigners, old age and suffering were depicted in a realistic way.

Terracottas

Terracottas are small statues made of baked clay. The early ones were made individually, but later some were made in moulds. Terracottas were brightly painted and were usually made as offerings to the gods or the dead. Here is a selection, ranging from the early, rather stiff looking figures, to the later ones, some of which show everyday scenes.

Metalwork

Gold, silver, bronze and iron were used to make a wide range of tableware, jewellery, weapons and other objects. Goods made by Greek craftsmen were in great demand abroad, and have been found by archaeologists all over Europe, South Russia and in the Near and Middle East.

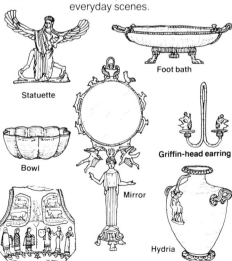

Statuette

Foot bath

Bowl

Mirror

Griffin-head earring

Hydria

Diadem

Breast plate

Learning and Inventions

Greek scholars looked into all aspects of the world around them. The Greeks called these scholars philosophers, although they studied subjects which we would divide into different categories, such as mathematics, astronomy, geology, or medicine. Some of their ideas were based on those of older civilizations, but they also made new and original discoveries, some of which provide the foundations for what we learn today.

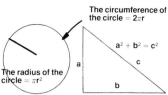

The circumference of the circle = $2\pi r$

The radius of the circle = πr^2

$a^2 + b^2 = c^2$

The greatest mathematicians were Pythagoras, Euclid and Archimedes. They worked out rules in geometry, such as Pythagoras's theorem on triangles and the "*pi*" theorem.

The Greeks studied the stars. This led one scholar to realize that the Earth floated freely in space. Older theories had suggested that it needed something to hold it up.

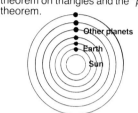

Other planets
Earth
Sun

The astronomer Aristarchus deduced that the Earth turned on its axis, while it and the other planets revolved round the sun.

A later Greek scholar, Ptolemy, believed that the Earth was the centre of the universe, as shown in this diagram. His theory was accepted until the 16th century.

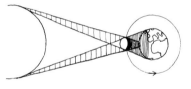

Another Greek put forward the correct explanation for eclipses, and the great scholar Thales was said to have predicted the solar eclipse of 585BC.

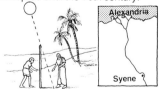

Alexandria

Syene

Eratosthenes worked out the distance round the Earth to within 200 miles. He did this by measuring the angle of the sun at Alexandria, and the distance from Alexandria to Syene, where the sun was overhead at noon.

This is a reconstruction of an astronomical clock, which was found on a wrecked ship. It helped sailors to plot the movements of the sun, moon and stars.

Alexandrian inventions

Scientific progress was made by Greeks in Alexandria. This 120m tall lighthouse was designed and built there by architects using advanced engineering techniques. There were bronze mirrors at the top to reflect the light.

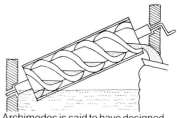

Archimedes is said to have designed this screw, a device for lifting water from one level to another. This method is still used today.

Alexandrian scholars carried out experiments to power machines by water and steam, but they were never put into use. This diagram shows a design for a water-driven clock.

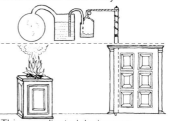

This complicated device was intended to make temple doors open when a fire was lit on the altar.

New tools and techniques

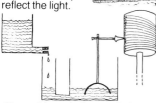

By the 2nd century BC, a new kind of anchor had been developed, that would hold firm even in very rough seas.

An improvement in the design of the potter's wheel allowed the potter to turn the wheel with his foot.

The lathe was probably invented by a Greek. A piece of wood was rotated on a spindle by a man pulling a string, while another man cut the wood with a chisel.

Iron-working was made easier by the introduction of welding. This involved joining pieces of iron by heating them, and then hammering them together on an anvil.

Medicine

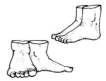

In early times, people tried to cure their illnesses with home-made remedies. If these failed, they might visit the temple of Asclepius, the god of medicine. By sleeping in the temple, the god or his snakes might appear in a dream to cure them. The priests also acted as doctors.

People who were cured sometimes made an offering in the form of a model of the cured part of the body.

Hippocrates

The founder of modern medicine is said to be Hippocrates of Cos, who lived in the 5th century BC. He and his followers saw that diseases had natural causes and were not sent by the gods as punishments. They stressed the importance of finding out all about the patient and his symptoms, in order to provide the correct diagnosis and treatment.

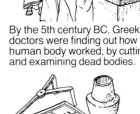

By the 5th century BC, Greek doctors were finding out how the human body worked, by cutting up and examining dead bodies.

Greek doctors prescribed herbal medicines, as well as rest and exercise. This drawing is from a manuscript giving recipes for medicines made from plants.

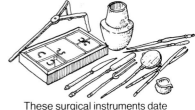

These surgical instruments date from the Hellenistic Period. Without modern drugs to kill pain and germs, operations were painful and dangerous. They were avoided whenever possible.

Studying fossils

Rich people paid to have the doctor of their choice. There were also some doctors paid for by the state, so that the poor could be treated free of charge.

Scholars studied the fossils of sea creatures found on land and deduced that the land had once been covered by sea. They concluded that all creatures, including humans, were descended from fish-like creatures.

Writers and Writing

The alphabet

Greek letter		Name of letter	English equivalent
A	α	alpha	a
B	β	beta	b
Γ	γ	gamma	g
Δ	δ	delta	d
E	ε	epsilon	e
Z	ζ	zeta	z
H	η	eta	e
Θ	θ	theta	th
I	ι	iota	i
K	κ	kappa	k
Λ	λ	lambda	l
M	μ	mu	m
N	ν	nu	n
Ξ	ξ	xi	x (ks)
O	o	omicron	o
Π	π	pi	p
P	ρ	rho	r
Σ	σ	sigma	s
T	τ	tau	t
Y	υ	ypsilon	ü, y
Φ	φ	phi	ph
X	χ	chi	kh,ch
Ψ	ψ	psi	ps
Ω	ω	omega	o

Poetry

The poet Homer lived in the 9th century BC. He told the story of the Trojan Wars in his poems, the *Iliad* and the *Odyssey*. This kind of poetry is called epic poetry.

History

Herodotus is called "The Father of History", as he was the first writer to try to distinguish between fact and legend. In his nine books, the *Historiai**, he wrote about the Persian Wars and his own travels.

Chart of Greek writers and philosophers

Socrates	469-399BC	Philospher. He encouraged people to question all their beliefs.
Plato	428-348BC	Philosopher. He founded a famous school called the Academy. His writings include *Dialogues* and *The Republic*.
Aristotle	384-322BC	Philosopher. He was Plato's pupil and taught Alexander the Great for a time. His writings include *Politics*.
Aeschylus	525-456BC	Writer of Tragedies. The most famous is *The Oresteia*.
Sophocles	496-407BC	Writer of tragedies. His plays include *Antigone, Electra* and *Oedipus Rex*.
Euripides	485-406BC	Writer of tragedies.
Aristophanes	450-385BC	Writer of Comedies. His plays include *The Birds, The Frogs* and *The Wasps*.
Hesiod	8th century BC	Writer. Wrote a history of the gods and farming.
Thucydides	471-400BC	Historian. He wrote about the war between Athens and Sparta.

*Historiai means "enquiries".

Map of Ancient Greece

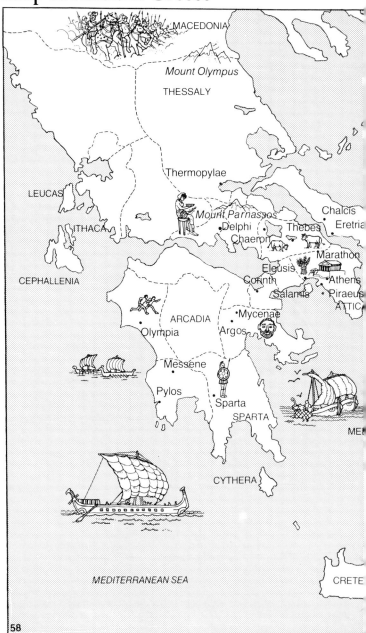

MACEDONIA

Mount Olympus

THESSALY

Thermopylae

LEUCAS

Mount Parnassos

ITHACA

Delphi

Chalcis

Thebes

Eretria

Chaeron

Marathon

CEPHALLENIA

Eleusis

Corinth

Athens

Salamis

Piraeus

ATTIC

ARCADIA

Mycenae

Olympia

Argos

Messene

Pylos

Sparta

SPARTA

MEL

CYTHERA

MEDITERRANEAN SEA

CRETE

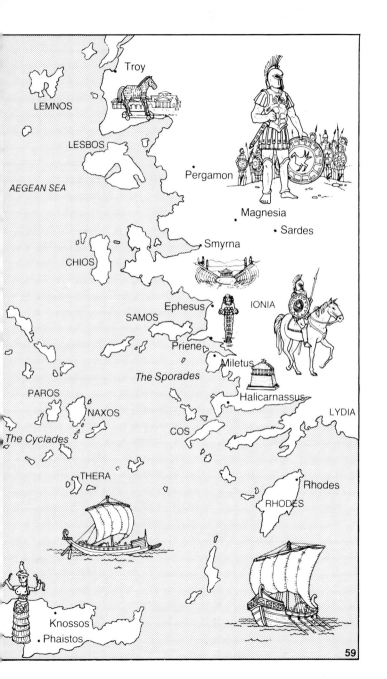

Troy

LEMNOS

LESBOS

AEGEAN SEA

Pergamon

Magnesia

Sardes

Smyrna

CHIOS

Ephesus

IONIA

SAMOS

Priene

Miletus

The Sporades

Halicarnassus

PAROS

LYDIA

NAXOS

COS

The Cyclades

THERA

Rhodes

RHODES

Knossos

Phaistos

The History of Ancient Greece

The earliest inhabitants of Greece were Stone Age hunters. Farming began in about 6000BC. Archaeologists divide the earliest civilizations into Helladic (mainland Greece), Cycladic (the Aegean Islands) and Minoan (Crete).

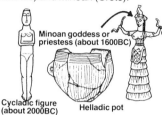

Cycladic figure (about 2000BC)

Minoan goddess or priestess (about 1600BC)

Helladic pot

Between 2200 and 1900BC, people who appear to have spoken an early form of Greek started arriving in Greece. A great civilization grew up, which we name after the city of Mycenae, and which lasted from about 1600 to 1100BC. The Trojan War took place towards the end of this period.

The Dark Ages

Gold mask (about 1500BC)

The period known as the Dark Ages began in about 1100BC. Greece was beset by troubles. The Mycenaeans lost control and a people, called the Dorians, invaded from the north.

During this period, the poet Homer composed *The Iliad* and *The Odyssey*. In the 8th century BC, the Greeks adopted a new, simple alphabet. The population increased and some people emigrated and set up colonies around the Mediterranean.

The Archaic Period

The Archaic Period was a time of political change. Kings had been replaced in power by nobles, who set up oligarchies. In many states, the oligarchies were then overthrown by tyrants, supported by the people. In 594BC, Solon, the ruler of Athens, granted a constitution which marked the first step towards democracy.

The Classical Period

The Classical Period is the time when Athens was at the height of its power. In 499BC, Greek cities in Asia Minor rebelled against their Persian rulers. Athens sent help, but the revolt failed and the Persians declared war against Athens.

The first Persian invasion ended in their defeat at Marathon in 490BC. In 480BC, Sparta and its allies fought the Persians at Thermopylae, but were defeated. In the same year, the Athenians won a great naval victory over the Persians at Salamis. The wars came to an end in 479BC, when the Persians were beaten at Plataea.

In Athens, there followed a golden age in the arts and learning. Many of the finest sculptures and painted pots were produced during this period. Athens formed the Delian League with other Greek states and dominated Greece politically.

In 432BC, the building of the Parthenon in Athens was completed.

Between about 460 and 430BC, Athenian politics were influenced by the brilliant and popular politician, Perikles.

The Peloponnesian Wars were fought between Athens and Sparta from 431 to 404BC. Athens was defeated and the Spartans installed their own government, though democracy was soon restored. The philosopher, Socrates, was forced to commit suicide in 399BC by those seeking to blame someone for the misfortunes of Athens.

Peace did not return to Greece. In 371BC, the Thebans defeated the Spartans. Meanwhile, the power of King Philip of Macedon (above) was growing. He fought many battles and eventually united Greece under his rule.

The Hellenistic Period

In 336BC, Philip was assassinated and succeeded by his son, Alexander the Great (336-323BC). Alexander conquered a vast empire, stretching from Egypt to India. In 331BC, the city of Alexandria was founded in Egypt and it became a centre of learning. After Alexander's death, his generals fought each other and divided the empire between them.

By this time, the Romans were beginning to acquire their own empire. First they took over the Greek colonies in Italy, then moved into Greece itself. Many Greeks were taken to Italy as slaves, and by 146BC, Greece had become a Roman province.

Museums and Sites

Here are the names of some museums where you can find interesting collections of Ancient Greek objects.

Australia

National Gallery of Victoria, **Melbourne**, Victoria.
Nicholson Museum of Antiquities, University of Sydney, **Sydney**, New South Wales.

Canada

Royal Ontario Museum, University of Toronto, **Toronto,** Ontario.

United Kingdom

Birmingham City Museum and Art Gallery, **Birmingham.**
Fitzwilliam Museum, **Cambridge.**
University Museum of Classical Archaeology, **Cambridge.**
Royal Scottish Museum, **Edinburgh.**
City Museum, **Leeds.**
City Museum, **Liverpool.**
British Museum, **London.**
Greek Museum, University of Newcastle, **Newcastle-upon-Tyne.**
Ashmolean Museum, **Oxford.**
Museum of Greek Archaeology, University of Reading, Whiteknights, **Reading.**

United States

John Hopkins Archaeological Collection, **Baltimore,** Maryland.
Walters Art Gallery, **Baltimore,** Maryland.
Palestine Institute Museum, Pacific School of Religion, **Berkeley,** California.
Indiana University Art Museum, **Bloomington,** Indiana.
Museum of Fine Arts, **Boston,** Massachusetts.
Bowdoin College Museum of Art, **Brunswick,** Maine.
J. Paul Getty Museum, **Malibu,** California.

Isaac Delgado Museum of Art, **New Orleans,** Louisiana.
Metropolitan Museum of Art, **New York,** New York.
Pierpont Morgan Library, **New York,** New York.
Walter Baker Collection, **New York,** New York.
Chrysler Art Museum, **Provincetown,** Massachusetts.
Santa Barbara Museum of Art, **Santa Barbara,** California.
Dumbarton Oaks Foundation, **Washington D.C.**

Ancient Greek sites

On the mainland and islands of Greece and parts of Turkey, you can still see Ancient Greek ruins. Here are the names of some places with interesting sites to visit.

Greece

Aegina
Athens
Bassae
Corinth
Delos (island of Delos)
Delphi
Dodona
Eleusis
Epidauros
Knossos (island of Crete)
Mycenae
Olympia
Olynthos
Sounion
Thera (island of Santorini)

Turkey

Miletus
Ephesus
Pergamon
Priene

Index